Pe...

Co...

Afghanistan

by Christine Juarez

Consulting Editor: Gail Saunders-Smith, PhD

CAPSTONE PRESS
a capstone imprint

Pebble Books are published by Capstone Press,
1710 Roe Crest Drive, North Mankato, Minnesota 56003
www.capstonepub.com

Library of Congress Cataloging-in-Publication Data
Juarez, Christine, 1976–
  Afghanistan / by Christine Juarez.
    pages cm.—(Pebble books. Countries)
  Includes bibliographical references and index.
  Summary: "Simple text and full-color photographs illustrate the land, animals, and people of
Afghanistan"—Provided by publisher.
  ISBN 978-1-4765-3518-0 (paperback)
1. Afghanistan—Juvenile literature. I. Title.
  DS351.5.J83 2014
  958.1—dc23   2013001981

Editorial Credits
Erika L. Shores, editor; Bobbie Nuytten, designer; Wanda Winch, media researcher;
Jennifer Walker, production specialist

Photo Credits
Capstone: 4 (globe); Corbis: National Geographic Society/Alex Treadway, 17, Reuters/Sultan
al Fahed, 15; Dreamstime: Bruno Pagnanelli, 5; iStockphoto: Christophe Cerisier, 1, 11, 21, Ivan
Vrhnjak, Jr., 13; Newscom: DanitaDelimont.com/"Danita Delimont Photography/Kenneth
Garrett, 19; Shutterstock: ayzek, 22 (flag), Godruma, cover (design), lebedev, cover, Nikm, 7,
Ohmega1982, back cover globe, Pim Leijen, 9, Robert Brown Stock, 22 (currency), skvoor, 4
(Afghanistan outline map)

Note to Parents and Teachers

The Countries set supports national social studies standards related
to people, places, and culture. This book describes and illustrates
Afghanistan. The images support early readers in understanding the text.
The repetition of words and phrases helps early readers learn new words.
This book also introduces early readers to subject-specific vocabulary
words, which are defined in the Glossary section. Early readers may need
assistance to read some words and to use the Table of Contents, Glossary,
Read More, Internet Sites, and Index sections of the book.

Printed in the United States of America in North Mankato, Minnesota.
032013   007223CGF13

Table of Contents

Where Is Afghanistan?

Afghanistan is a country
in southern Asia. It is about
the size of the U.S. state of Texas.
Afghanistan's capital is Kabul.

Kabul ★

AFGHANISTAN

Landforms and Climate

Rugged mountains cover half
of Afghanistan. Plains are
found in northern parts of
the country. Afghanistan has
cold winters and hot summers.

Animals

Afghanistan's mountains are home to many wild animals. There are foxes, wolves, and striped hyenas. Wild goats and brown bears also roam the country.

Language and Population

About 31 million people live
in Afghanistan. Most Afghans
live in the countryside.
Pashto and Dari are Afghanistan's
official languages.

Food

Rice, naan, and yogurt are the main foods eaten by Afghans. Naan is a type of flat bread. Rice is served with beef or lamb stews. Tea is the most popular drink.

Celebrations

Most Afghans are Muslims.
Muslims celebrate Islamic holidays.
The month of Ramadan is important
to Muslims. Most people fast
from sunup to sundown.

Where People Work

Most Afghans are farmers.

They grow wheat, corn, and rice.

Some farmers raise sheep

for their wool and meat.

17

Transportation

Few Afghans own cars. Afghans travel in carts pulled by donkeys or horses. They also walk or ride bicycles or buses. Rural Afghans ride donkeys, camels, or horses.

19

Famous Sight

Band-I Amir National Park
has six dark blue lakes.
Visitors use paddleboats.
People have picnics along
the shores.

Country Facts

Name: Islamic Republic of Afghanistan

Capital: Kabul

Population: 31,108,077 (July 2013 estimate)

Size: 251,827 square miles
(652,230 square kilometers)

Languages: Pashto and Dari. Other languages are spoken locally.

Main Crops: wheat, fruits, nuts

Money: Afghani

Afghanistan's flag

22

Glossary

Asia—the largest continent on Earth; Afghanistan is in southern Asia

capital—the city in a country where the government is based

fast—to give up eating for a period of time

language—the way people speak or talk

Muslim—a person who follows the religion of Islam; Islam is based on the teachings of Muhammad

naan—a type of flat bread

official—having the approval of a country or a certain group of people

plain—a large, flat area of land

popular—liked or enjoyed by many people

Ramadan—an Islamic religious holiday when Muslims fast

rural—having to do with the countryside

Hirsch, Rebecca. *Asia.* Rookie Read-About Geography. New York: Children's Press, 2012.

Owings, Lisa. *Afghanistan.* Exploring Countries. Minneapolis: Bellwether Media, 2011.

Spilsbury, Richard. *Discover Afghanistan.* Discover Countries. New York: PowerKids Press, 2012.

Internet Sites

FactHound offers a safe, fun way to find Internet sites related to this book. All of the sites on FactHound have been researched by our staff.

Here's all you do:
Visit *www.facthound.com*
Type in this code: 9781476530789

Super-cool stuff!

Check out projects, games and lots more at
www.capstonekids.com

Index